4 95

An Approach to Vedanta

An Approach to Vedanta

Christopher Isherwood

Vedanta Press

International Standard Book Number 0-87481-003-5 Second edition, 1981
10 9 8 7 6 5 4 3 2

Printed in the United States of America

Those who wish to learn in greater detail about the teachings contained in
this book are invited to write to the Secretary, Vedanta Society of Southern
California, 1946 Vedanta Place, Hollywood, CA 90068.

Foreword

IN FEBRUARY 1958 I was about to start writing a biography of Ramakrishna.

I decided that I would have to begin with a few chapters of autobiography, explaining how I personally came to hear about Ramakrishna and was drawn to become his devotee. This was how I reasoned: I had made my first contact with Ramakrishna through a person, not through a book. My approach to him had been that of getting to know the friend of a friend, as it were; an emotional rather than an intellectual experience. Therefore, I could only describe this experience to others in the form of a personal statement.

Having decided this, I set to work and wrote the pages which follow. But, when I had finished them, I saw that I had been wrong. As an introduction to a Ramakrishna biography they were unsuitable, for two reasons: I seemed to be pushing my own personality between Ramakrishna and the reader; and my explanations of Hindu philosophical theories and beliefs were ill-timed—they should have been fed to the reader little by little at appropriate points in Ramakrishna's story, not crammed down his throat in one huge meal before the story had even begun.

So I tried again—starting the biography right away, without any autobiographical introduction.

Not long ago, however, I reread this manuscript and then showed it to friends. We decided that it might be worth publishing separately, as a greatly expanded version of my essay in the symposium *What Vedanta Means to Me*. You will find some ideas and phrases from that essay here; also from an essay called "The Gita and War" which is included in the Prabhavananda-Isherwood translation of the Bhagavad-Gita. Otherwise, this material is almost altogether new. I have made a few cuts and alterations, to correct it and bring it up to date.

1.

TOWARD the end of January 1939, I arrived with W. H. Auden
in New York by boat from England.

Why had I come to America? I suppose because I couldn't
stop traveling; I had become constitutionally restless. The mech-
anism had been set going during the six years since Hitler's
seizure of power and my consequent departure from Germany,
which I had almost begun to regard as home; six years of wan-
dering around Western Europe from Sweden to Spain, ending
up with a trip to China with Auden in 1938. And now America
was the obvious next move. We had had a brief, melodramatic
glimpse of it the previous summer, on our way home from the
Far East. We had shot up and down skyscrapers, in and out of
parties and bars; we had watched a fight in a Bowery dive, heard
Maxine Sullivan sing in Harlem, been at Coney Island on July
the Fourth. I had gone back to England raving about Manhattan,
convinced, like most tourists, that New York is the United
States.

However, the Christopher who now returned to New York
was no longer quite the same Christopher who had left it five
months before. For one thing, I had just realized—while we
were crossing the Atlantic—that I was a pacifist.

Maybe it would be more exact to say: I realized that I had
always been a pacifist. At any rate, in the negative sense. How
could I have ever imagined that I was anything else? My earliest
remembered feelings of rebellion were against the British Army,
in which my father was a regular officer, and against the staff of
my first boarding school, who tried, with the best intentions, to
make me believe in a glamorized view of the 1914-18 War and
of my father's death in it. My father had taught me, by his life
and death, to hate the profession of soldiering. I remember his
telling me, before he left for France, that an officer's sword is
useless except for toasting bread, and that he never fired his
revolver because he couldn't hit anything with it and hated the

bang. He was killed while leading an attack, carrying only a swagger stick with which he was signaling directions to his men. I adored my father's memory, dwelling always on his civilian virtues; his gentleness, his humor, his musical and artistic talent. Growing up into the postwar world, I learnt to loathe the old men who had made the war. Flags, uniforms and war memorials made me tremble with rage because they filled me with terror. I was horribly scared by the idea of War and therefore subconsciously attracted to it.

However, in 1936, a war broke out which seemed, at first, to present a clear-cut issue between right and wrong: the Civil War in Spain. I joined my friends—and the vast majority of English writers—in supporting the Republican Government. We believed that the Government, being absolutely in the right, was entitled to use any means available to overcome its enemies. So my pacifism was temporarily forgotten. And, like my friends, I greeted the entry of Soviet Russia into the Popular Front as an ally, even though most of us had been shocked by the injustice shown in the Moscow treason trials of the early thirties.

Auden had already visited Spain, early in the war. Toward the end of 1937, I arranged to go with him to Madrid, as part of a delegation of English writers and artists sympathetic to the Government cause. But this visit was repeatedly postponed by the Spanish authorities, and in the meantime Auden and I had been offered a contract by our publishers to write a book about any country in the Far East. So we decided to leave in January 1938 for China. China had lately been invaded by the Japanese and was in a situation somewhat similar to that of Spain; a (more or less) democratic Government attacked by unprovoked aggressors.

I have already indicated one of my motives for wanting to get into a ringside seat at a war: the fascination of one's own fear, a motive many people must have for going big game hunting. Also, of course, there was ordinary healthy excitement and wanderlust. Also, there was genuine concern for the victims of aggression and a desire to make their wrongs known to the rest of the world—yes, there was a little, at least, of that too.

As a matter of fact, our visit to wartime China did me a great deal of good. First, it reduced my neurotic fear of War in the abstract. True, our journey through the combat zone wasn't really very dangerous. I think there were only three or four occasions on which we were at all likely to have been killed by bombs or bullets. But a very little danger will go a long way, psychologically. Several times I was afraid, but only healthily afraid. I now no longer dreaded some unknown horror, or feared that I should behave much worse than other people in the same circumstances.

Secondly, the visit to China brought me back from a world of political principles to a world of human values which I had temporarily lost. In China I saw boys in their early teens who had been conscripted to serve in the front-line trenches. I saw the corpses of old men and women killed in an air raid. I smelled the rotting bodies of wounded soldiers dying of gas gangrene. War starts with principles but it ends with people—people who have usually little or no interest in the principles. This was an obvious fact which I had been overlooking; and nothing hits you harder than the obvious, when you suddenly become aware of it. I found I didn't dare to say that these people ought to die in defense of any principles whatsoever, no matter how noble or right. In fact, balanced against this suffering and death, all such questions of right and wrong seemed academic and irrelevant. My own acceptance of armed force as a means of political action had been due simply to a lack of feeling and imagination. *That* I knew was true—at least as far as I myself was concerned. I couldn't speak for others. If they honestly believed in the rightness of fighting, *and* were prepared to prove their honesty by risking their own lives, then I would honor them and try to imitate their courage in following my own path. But for the future I myself must be an avowed pacifist.

(I must pause here to make one point as clear as I can. In this statement, I am not trying to present a general case in favor of pacifism. I am describing my own feelings as they related to a series of situations; and I am only doing this in order to explain how they brought me into touch with the ideas of Vedanta. Therefore, it is useless for the reader to ask me indignantly, "Can you pretend that you would still be a pacifist if you belonged to a racial minority threatened with extermination?" I can't tell him. I haven't been in that situation. So I don't know.) Such was my decision, as it finally became clear to me. But for a while nothing was clear. The autumn of 1938 was a period of confusion for all of us. There was the climax and anticlimax of Munich. There was the tragedy of the crumbling of the Spanish Government, destroyed from within quite as much as from without; allies accusing each other of treason and the clear-seeming lines of political integrity becoming more and more distorted. There was the emerging possibility of almost indefinite Nazi expansion without general war.

Clear thinking was impossible during the Munich crisis. It was impossible as long as I was lecturing to audiences on our Chinese journey, and thereby identifying myself with China's armed resistance to the Japanese invasion. But the voyage to New York provided a break for thought in the midst of all this compulsive activity. I had time to ask myself where I stood.

Thus I accepted the fact that I was a pacifist. If War came, I would refuse to fight. That was all I had left to go on with: a negation. For, as I now began to realize, my whole political position, left-wing anti-fascist, had been based on the acceptance of armed force. All the slogans I had been repeating and living by were essentially militaristic. Very well: throw them out. But what remained? I told myself that I should have to put my emotions back from a political on to a personal basis. I would be an individual again, with my own values, my own kind of integrity. This sounded challenging and exciting. But it raised a disconcerting question: what were the values to be?

In the mid-1920's, when I was a very young man, I had taken as my ideal the figure of The Artist, as it is presented by the romantic writers of the nineteenth century. The Artist stands alone; this is his tragedy and his glory. He is isolated from the common crowd by the superior fineness of his perceptions. His work is therefore generally misunderstood and condemned. He is scorned, persecuted, let starve, sometimes even imprisoned or put to death. All this he suffers, because he refuses to disguise the truth as he sees it. Baudelaire, in his famous poem, compares The Poet to an albatross whose giant wings prevent him from walking on the ground which symbolizes dull common everyday life. He is presented as a dedicated and holy figure—a martyr and in his own way a saint.

Later, at the beginning of the 1930's, I passed, like most of my friends, into a socially-conscious political phase. What were important, we now declared, were the needs and wrongs of the common man. The function of art was to proclaim them. We wanted to expose abuses and denounce tyrants and exploiters. We wanted to point the way to a happier era of peace and plenty, equality and civil justice. We were utopian socialists. If our critics called us propagandists, we agreed with them proudly. "All Art is propaganda," we replied. "Intentionally or unintentionally, it is bound to express some kind of a philosophy, either reactionary or progressive. The merit we claim for *our* propaganda is that it is both progressive and intentional."

Since we were concerned with the common man and the welfare of the exploited many, we were unavoidably critical and hostile in our attitude toward the few. Everything uncommon and private had become suspect by us. We now sneered at the romantic ideal of The Artist. His private sensibilities and his alienation from the masses no longer impressed us; we had decided that his predicament was merely due to neurosis.

Such had been my philosophy during the 1930's. Now I was discarding it in favor of some kind of individualism, at present ill-defined. It seemed to me that I knew only what I *didn't* want, what I *couldn't* accept.

I couldn't accept, any longer, this attitude of self-abasement before the concepts of the Masses and the Common Man; it now seemed to me masochistic and insincere. It seemed to me that I had been confusing a valid concern for the victims of injustice with an invalid and almost idolatrous cult of the majority *as* a majority. As a matter of fact, I didn't like or respect majorities or believe that they must necessarily be in the right: I only feared them, and therefore wished to propitiate them. As for the Common Man (if such a being exists) I didn't honestly think that he must always be possessed of a superior wisdom about life. I was still ready to admit that there might be things he could teach me, but I now cast false humility aside and claimed that there were things I could teach *him*. Why should either of us humble himself before the other?

But though I was proposing to live a less political and more personal life, I couldn't, ever again, be an individualist in the old sense. I had discovered that I had been too much involved in politics, or involved in the wrong way; but I knew that I must never dare to ignore what was going on in the world around me. And whenever I met social injustice on the personal level, I must try to take up its challenge.

Moreover, I couldn't any longer accept The Artist as my ideal—for, as I now realized, I no longer believed in Art as an absolute aim and justification of a human life. Certainly I still intended to write books; but writing, in itself, wasn't enough for me. It might occupy most of my time, but it couldn't be my means of spiritual support, my religion.

Religion! How the word still made me wince and grit my teeth with loathing! I had declared myself an atheist at the age of twenty and now, at nearly thirty-five, I hadn't changed my opinion. I had no expectation that I should ever do so. Religion, I was prepared to tell all and sundry, was evil, superstitious reactionary nonsense, and those who propagated it were enemies of progress and of mankind.

But what did I mean by "religion"?

By "religion" I meant the Christian religion as I had encountered it through the Church of England, into which I had been baptized as a baby and confirmed as a teen-age boy. I regarded the Hindus, Buddhists and Mohammedans as picturesque heathens merely. I didn't think of them as being "religious" at all.

I hated Christianity—the kind of Christianity I had been taught—because it was dualistic. God, high in heaven, ruled with grim justice over us, his sinful and brutish subjects, here below. He was good. We were bad. We were so bad that we crucified Jesus his son, whom he had sent down to live amongst us. For this crime, committed nearly two thousand years ago, each new generation had to beg forgiveness. If we begged hard enough and were sincerely sorry, we might be sent to purgatory and even eventually let into heaven, instead of being thrown into hell where we by rights belonged.

Who—I furiously exclaimed—wouldn't rebel against the concept of such a God? Who wouldn't abhor his tyranny? Who wouldn't denounce the cruel unfairness of this test he had set us: one short human life in which to earn salvation or damnation? Who wouldn't detest his Son, who had come to us—like a vice squad officer bent on entrapment—wearing a hypocritical mask of meekness in order to tempt us to murder him? Such were the questions I asked; and my answer was that only slaves could accept such a religion. In the Christian hell one could expect to meet every honest and courageous man or woman who had ever lived. If hell existed, then I for one would be proud to be damned.

But hell, I added, *didn't* exist. And neither did God, with his laws and his punishments. The whole thing was, only too obviously, a fiction invented by schoolmasters and policemen; a projection of their own morbid guilt-complexes and life-hatred.

When I looked at the Christians around me, I chose to see them as a collection of dreary canting hypocrites, missionaries of ignorance and reaction, who opposed all social reform lest it should endanger the status and privileges of their Church, and all personal freedom lest the individual should discover for himself that the "don'ts" they preached were unnecessary. I loathed their gravity, their humility, their lack of humor, their special tone when speaking of their God. I believed, or pretended to believe, that every Christian was secretly longing to indulge in forbidden pleasures, and that he was only prevented from doing so by his cowardice, ugliness or impotence. I delighted in stories which told of clergymen being seduced, and monks and nuns carrying on clandestine love affairs. My malice against them knew no bounds. At the same time, I proudly declared that I myself needed no religion to keep me moral, according to my own standards. I tried to behave more or less decently because I freely chose to follow the advice of my own conscience; *I* didn't need the Ten Commandments to nudge me, or the fear of an absurd mediaeval nightmare called Hell.

I have no doubt that these exaggerated reactions were, to some extent, produced by certain experiences in my boyhood which had given me a dread of authority. Certainly, my violence on this subject approached hysteria. But this isn't important, as far as my present narrative is concerned. For my prejudices, neurotic though they may have been, had also a relation to the reasonable criticisms which can be made of conventional Christianity. They were by no means utterly unjustified. And they had to be reasonably dealt with before I could get out of my philosophical dead end, and find myself another road.

THIS second visit of mine to New York was a disaster, almost from the start. The conquering confident mood in which I had approached America quickly disappeared. It had been based on the illusions of a tourist, and now I was a tourist no longer. I wanted to make my own niche in American life, and settle down and get to work. But I found that I couldn't write a line. I was paralyzed by apprehension. The high cost of our living scared me. So did the European news, which got steadily worse; until war seemed almost inevitable. The hospitality of friends and strangers couldn't reassure me, for I felt that I was accepting it under false pretences. The Christopher Isherwood they wanted to see was no longer myself—for he represented those very attitudes and beliefs I had just abandoned. For the same reason, I was most unwilling to teach or give lectures: I could no longer tell an audience the things they expected to hear from me—and I certainly couldn't appear before them with a new "message." There was no conceivable statement I could venture to make at this point in my life, except "I don't know."

As the weeks went by, my sense of insecurity became more and more acute. I began to realize that, whatever else I did, I must get away from New York. In New York, I was, to a minor degree, a public figure—and one which had, in reality, ceased to exist. Now I desperately needed anonymity, time to think, and someone to help me do my thinking. Where should I go? Who would help me?

I HAD first met Gerald Heard in London in 1930. At that time, his chief interests were prehistory, the evolution of man, the advances of modern science on its various fronts, and the investigation of psychic phenomena. He had written a number of books, but his friends agreed that his greatest brilliance was shown in his lectures, radio-talks and conversation. He had, and has, a genius for communicating to others the fervor of his own interest in any subject he discusses.

In 1937, Gerald Heard, Aldous and Maria Huxley and a close friend of mine named Christopher Wood had all left England and settled in California, in the Los Angeles area. Rumors had reached us that Gerald was now devoting himself to the study of Yoga. My friends and I had laughed over this; we pictured him levitating with Huxley in turbans and floating out over the desert at a great altitude. But the rumor, even if true, didn't at all shake my faith in Gerald's basic integrity. It seemed right for him to be investigating any kind of esoteric lore, the more disreputable the better. For he had the curiosity of the truly intelligent, combined with a sane scepticism which isn't afraid to find mud around the well of truth. The fact that some mediums are fakes had never driven him into the ranks of those intellectual cowards who—largely because of their terror of being laughed at—denounce psychical research as mere self-deception. If Gerald was temporarily interested in these yogis, or yogas, or swamis, or whatever they were called—then good luck to him, I said. I knew that his findings would at any rate make an excellent story, because Gerald is one of the greatest story-tellers alive.

It was not as a yoga-adept, however, that I now appealed to him, but as a pacifist. Both he and Aldous Huxley had already declared their pacifism in various books and articles. We exchanged letters. Gerald wrote that "every pacifist should acquire medical knowledge . . . creative accuracy must be opposed to disorder and destruction . . . we must create a doctorate of psychologically sound, well-equipped healers." This sounded authoritative and encouraging, even if somewhat vague. I certainly knew that I needed discipline of some kind in my own life—and the idea of being a healer, in whatever sense, appealed to me, who had once seriously considered becoming a doctor.

And thus I decided to leave for California. I wanted to have some long talks with Gerald and find out exactly what he meant, and what he had discovered. I wanted to hear from Christopher Wood—an Englishman of my own age, with whom I could closely identify myself—how he had managed to settle down and adjust to American life. I wanted to meet Aldous and Maria Huxley. And then there was my ever itching wanderlust. The "real" America of my daydreams had always been the Far West. Wishing to see the country through the eyes of one of its natives, I persuaded a young footloose artist to come with me. We set off early in May, with very little money, on a Greyhound Bus.

In contrast with New York, Hollywood (where we first settled) seemed a sanctuary—simply because of the presence of my friends. Chris Wood reassured me just as I had hoped he would, by helping me over the difficult period of getting accustomed to this familiar-foreign land. He also took away most of my material worries, by lending me enough money to live on until I eventually got work as a movie-writer. And as for Gerald, he did indeed answer many of my questions—and, at the same time, caused me to ask twice as many new ones.

I have difficulty at this point in my narrative because I must now try to tell in a logical, tidy way what it was that Gerald had to say to me. I must begin at the beginning. But such dialogues between human beings—carried on throughout a series of meetings and over a period of months—never do begin at the beginning or end at the end. They jump from topic to topic, turn around upon themselves, are inconsequent and repetitious. Therefore I must present what follows in a falsely stylized and simplified manner.

This is *not* the story of a conversion through intellectual conviction. Is anyone ever convinced of anything by pure reason alone? Well, I suppose it is possible that pure reason could lead you to choose one make of electric toaster out of several. But that is, surely, never the way in which the decisive convictions of our lives are arrived at. The right teacher must appear at exactly the right moment in the right place; and his pupil must be in the right mood to accept what he teaches. Then—and only then—can argument and reason exert their full power. Surely we can all agree on that? And yet so many autobiographers distort their narratives by presenting themselves as creatures who make all decisions rationally and change their opinions just because they have been intellectually convinced that they should do so! I hope to avoid that error here.

I must start, then, by making it clear that I put Gerald—not once but over and over again during the months that followed—to the test of my intuition—not an infallible test, to be sure, but, in the long run, the best that any of us can settle for, short of mathematical certainty. Watching him carefully—making all due allowance for his love of arresting phrases and ingenious analogies, and for the powerfully persuasive beauty of his voice —I had to say to myself: No, he isn't lying, either to me or to himself. And he isn't crazy. I know this man. He speaks the same language I do. He accepts the same values. If this is true for him, then I'm forced to admit that it must be true for me, too.

Although I had just traveled three thousand miles to see Gerald, this was still a disturbing thought: that, if Gerald *was* sane, I couldn't afford to ignore his ideas. I should have to study them, perhaps act on them. Gerald, I could see, was expecting that I should. He had the air of having waited for my arrival as one waits for a valuable recruit—an assistant, almost. Very few people, he flatteringly hinted, ever came to "this thing" (his favorite synonym for the matter of his investigations). Only one man in ten thousand would take an interest at all. And of those ten thousand, only one would do anything about it. "It's only when the sheer *beastliness* of the world begins to hurt you—like crushing your finger in a door—it's only then that you'll be ready to take this step."

What step?

I can't exactly remember, after all these years, just what it was that I had expected Gerald to be doing—what I had supposed "Yoga" to be all about. Some kind of ritualistic practices, no doubt, partaking of black magic, along with a study of the cabala (whatever that was), crystal-gazing, tarot pack reading and maybe some breathing exercises which would enable one, when sufficiently adept, to be buried alive. Probably, I hadn't bothered to picture anything clearly. I had merely sneered.

This "Yoga" in which Gerald was so passionately interested had, I now learned, nothing whatsoever to do with fortune-telling, scrying or casting spells. A small branch of it, called Hatha Yoga, did, it was true, deal in breathing exercises—but Gerald didn't practice these. The Swami was against them. He said they were dangerous if carried to excess and might lead to hallucinations.

("Who is 'the Swami'?" I asked. "Swami Prabhavananda," Gerald answered, "I want you to meet him soon.")

Gerald explained that yoga is a Sanskrit word—the ancestor of our English word "yoke"—and that it means, basically, "union." Yoga is a method—any one of many methods—by which the individual can achieve union with God.

(Probably, Gerald never actually used the word "God" during this first stage of my indoctrination. He was wise enough to avoid it—knowing only too well from his own experience how repulsive it must be to a refugee from Christian dualism like myself. Besides, "God" in the Yoga sense is a quite different concept from that of "God" in the Christian sense. But more of that, later.)

Yoga philosophy teaches that we have two selves—an apparent, outer self and an invisible, inner self. The apparent self claims to be an individual and as such, other than all other individuals. It calls itself by a name, seeks its own advantage, is anxious, cheerful, afraid, bold, lustful, enraged, hungry, thirsty, sleepy, cold, hot, healthy, sick, young or old, as the ever altering case may be. The real self is unchanging and immortal; it has no individuality, for it is equally within every human being, living creature, vegetable, mineral and inanimate object. Or, to put it in another way, there is a part of myself which, being infinite, has access to the infinite—as the sea water in a bay has access to the sea because it *is* the sea.

Therefore, Yoga is the process of exploring your own nature; of finding out what it really is. It is the process of becoming aware of your real situation. The day-to-day space-time "reality" (as it is reported to us by our senses and the daily newspapers) is, in fact, no reality at all, but a deadly and cunning illusion. The practice of yoga meditation consists in excluding, as far as possible, our consciousness of the illusory world, the surface "reality," and turning the mind inward in search of its real nature. Our real nature is to be one with life, with consciousness, with everything else in the universe. The fact of oneness is the real situation. Supposed individuality, separateness and division are merely illusion and ignorance. Awareness is increased through love (or, as Gerald preferred to call it, "interest-affection") and weakened by hatred; since love strengthens the sense of oneness and hatred the sense of separateness. Hence all positive feeling and action toward other people is in one's deepest interests, and all negative feeling and action finally harm oneself.

It should be obvious, from the above, why Gerald had to be a pacifist; any support of military force, on his part—however partial or carefully qualified—would have been a denial of his basic beliefs. Nevertheless, Gerald's pacifism might well have been attacked by those pacifists who believe in political action

—demonstrations, hunger strikes and the tactics of nonviolence. Such people no doubt described him as a quietist, a too passive observer of the catastrophe toward which the world was heading. Throughout the 1939-45 war, Gerald was in fact always ready to offer sympathy and practical advice to those young conscientious objectors who had gotten into difficulties with the authorities; but he himself was by nature philosophically detached. He had little belief in the efficacy of political action. He was constantly reminding us that free will does not operate—as we wishfully imagine it does—in the sphere of present events; averting this danger, gaining that advantage. No—at any given moment of action, we are tied hand and foot, because our present problems are created by our past deeds and thoughts. We have to do whatever we have already made it inevitable that we shall do. In the sphere of events, we can affect the working out of the future; we can do nothing to touch the present moment. Free will, applied to the present moment, consists simply in this: no matter what is happening to us, we can, at any moment, turn away from or toward our real nature. We can deny its existence or affirm it. We can forget its presence or remember it. We can act and think in a way that will bring us closer to it or alienate us from it.

AND NOW—leaving theory and getting down to practice—how in fact are we to turn toward and affirm the existence of our real nature? In two ways, Gerald said. Firstly, by living in such a manner as to remove the obstacles to self-knowledge. Secondly, by the regular practice of meditation.

The obstacles to self-knowledge came under three heads— Gerald had a tidy mind and was apt to speak of the universal truths in terms of a filing-system—addictions, possessions and pretensions. Addictions (which included also aversions: anything from chain-smoking to a horror of cats) were, according to him, the least harmful of the three. Pretensions were the worst, because, when you are free of all sensual attachments and all your superfluous belongings, when you have forgiven all your

enemies and said good-bye to all your lovers, when you have
resigned from all your positions of honor and ceased to used
your titles of nobility—then, and only then, are you liable to fall
victim to the spiritual arrogance which can become the worst
obstacle of all.

Much of this "intentional living" (another of Gerald's
phrases) must obviously be negative in character, since it is
concerned with self-discipline. The positive side of one's effort
to gain self-knowledge was to be found in the practice of meditation. At this time, Gerald himself was meditating six hours a
day; two in the morning, two at noon, two at night. He made
light of this truly intimidating schedule, saying that it was really
a minimum, as far as he was concerned. If he didn't constantly
remind himself of "this thing" during at least six of his waking
hours, he feared that he would lose touch with it altogether. This
left the rest of us free to draw the obvious conclusion.

What did Gerald actually do when he meditated? What did
he think about? Gerald seemed unwilling to answer these questions very specifically. It was a private matter, I gathered. There
were no general rules. Each individual would arrive at his own
methods, in accordance with his own needs and temperament.
Gerald himself had his instructions from Swami Prabhavananda,
who would doubtless instruct me also if I asked him to do so. In
the meanwhile, until I had made up my mind to go seriously into
pursuit of "this thing," Gerald said it would do me no harm to
practice short "sits." I wasn't to set myself any programme of
meditation. I wasn't to *try* to meditate at all. I was merely to sit
quiet, for ten or fifteen minutes twice a day, morning and evening. I was to remind myself of "this thing," what it was and
why I wanted it.

This I said I would do—and I did do it, now and then. This
kind of playing at meditation filled me with an excitement
which I have seldom felt since. It was most exciting to sit on the
floor in a corner of the room, in the darkness of early morning or
evening, and feel that one was face to face with the unknown

that was oneself. This was a sort of flirtation with the unconscious—made exciting, like all flirtations, by the eventual possibility of "doing something about it."

And meanwhile I listened to Gerald's ideas with growing enthusiasm. What appealed to me so strongly in his teaching was its lack of dogmatism. "Try it and find out for yourself" was, in effect, what he was telling me. Previously, I had thought of "religion" in terms of dogmas, commandments and declarative statements—in terms, that is to say, of a Church. The Church presents it dogmatic ultimatum—"do this or be damned"—and you have to choose between accepting it in its entirety or rejecting it altogether. But what Gerald recommended was a practical mysticism, a do-it-yourself religion which was experimental and empirical. You were on your own, setting forth to find things out for yourself in your individual way. As a matter of historical fact, the Christian Church has always been somewhat unfriendly and suspicious in its attitude toward this kind of research, although it has been forced to admit from time to time that some of the researchers have been saints.

Gerald started out with a single proposition, which was actually no more than a working hypothesis: "The real self can be known." If you asked him what his authority was in making this statement, he would reply that it was the past experience of others—the great mystics such as Meister Eckhart, St. John of the Cross and Ramakrishna, who had achieved this ultimate self-knowledge. (Gerald's conversation was full of such names —so many of them, indeed, that I never got the opportunity to find out who all of them were, especially since Gerald always courteously assumed that you knew. Ramakrishna's was one of the most frequently mentioned. I realized, of course, that he was an East Indian; beyond that, I was pretty vague, confusing him, more or less, with Krishnamurti [whom Gerald and Huxley knew personally] and with Radhakrishnan, the great scholar who was later to become President of India!)

But Gerald was quick to add that he wasn't asking you to take anything on trust. It was essential to try "this thing" for yourself. If, after a reasonable time, you had found nothing, then you were entitled to say that it was all a lie—and that the great mystics were madmen or hypocrites. This was his challenge, and it seemed to me that nothing could be fairer. In my excitement and enthusiasm, I kept asking: why didn't anybody ever tell me this before? The question was, of course, unreasonable. I had been "told this" innumerable times. Every moment of my waking life had contained within itself this riddle "what is life for?" and its answer "to learn what life means." Every event, every person I had met, had presented or indirectly stated both question and answer in some new way. Only, I hadn't been ready to listen. Why I was now ready—despite all my laziness and hesitations—I have just tried to explain.

I was ready, but I think I might still have procrastinated for a long time, if it hadn't been for the pressure of outside events. "The sheer beastliness of the world," as Gerald had called it, became increasingly obvious as the summer advanced and the hope of peace grew smaller. It was a ghastly time for everybody —except I suppose for those who actually wanted the war to come. Like the millions of others who didn't, I felt sick with foreboding. I didn't know how the crisis would affect my own life or what I was going to do about it, but I did know that I must find some kind of strength and belief within myself. I couldn't face what was coming in a state of agnostic stoicism. Only the very brave can be stoics, and even they often end in suicide.

2.

AT LENGTH, toward the end of July, I asked Gerald to take me to visit Swami Prabhavananda. I had decided to ask the Swami to teach me meditation.

(The title of "Swami" has more or less the same significance as that of "Father" in the Catholic Church, and it can only be properly assumed by a bona fide Hindu monk. The vast majority of those who call themselves Swamis in this country—fortunetellers, mental healers and the like—have absolutely no right to do so. At the time of his initiation, the swami receives a new Sanskrit name. "Prabhavananda" means "one who finds bliss within the Source of all creation." "Ananda," meaning "bliss" or "peace," is the suffix usually attached to a swami's name.)

The Swami's home was in the hills above Hollywood. Although Hollywood Boulevard was only a few minutes' walk away, at the bottom of a steep hill, his street was then a very quiet one. (It has since been cut across by the freeway.) The Swami lived in a pleasant old wooden house on the corner. Right next door to this house was a squat white plaster Hindu temple, surmounted by three onion-domes whose pinnacles were painted gold. The temple stood at the top of two flights of brick steps, flanked by cypresses. The proportions of this layout were good; though so small, it was impressive.

The Swami, also, I found to be small and impressive. Not formidable. Not in the least severe or hypnotic or dignified. But very definitely and unobtrusively one who had the authority of personal experience. Outwardly, he was a Bengali in his middle forties who looked at least fifteen years younger, charming and boyish in manner, with bold straight eyebrows and dark wide-set eyes. He talked in a gentle, persuasive voice. His smile was extraordinary—so open, so brilliant with joy that it had a strange kind of poignancy which could make your eyes fill suddenly

with tears. Later, I got to know another look of his—an intro-
spective look which seemed to withdraw all life from the surface
of his face, leaving it quite bare and lonely, like the face of a
mountain.

During our first interview, I felt terribly awkward. Everything I said sounded artificial. I started acting a little scene,
trying to make myself appear sympathetic to him. I told him I
wasn't sure that I could meditate and at the same time lead a life
in "the world," earning my living writing movie scripts. He
answered: "You must be like the lotus on the pond. The lotus-
leaf is never wet."

I said I was afraid of attempting to do too much, because I
should be so discouraged if I failed. He said: "There is no failure
in the search for God. Every step you take is a positive advance."

I said I hated the word "God." He agreed that you could just
as well say "The Self."

I asked how one could be sure that meditation wasn't just a
process of autohypnosis. He replied: "Autohypnosis or auto-
suggestion makes you see what you want to see. Meditation
makes you see something you don't expect to see. Autosugges-
tion produces different results in each individual. Meditation
produces the same result in all individuals."

I told him that I had always thought of such practices as
nothing but a lot of mumbo jumbo. He laughed: "And now you
have fallen into the trap?"

I don't think he was exactly bored by all this, only quietly
aware of the futility of talk, at this point in the proceedings. So
he waited, patiently and politely, for my chattering to end. As
soon as I had taken at least one tiny step by myself, we would be
able to talk practice instead of theory.

THE SWAMI's first instructions to me were, briefly, as follows:
1. Try to feel, all around you, the presence of an all-pervading
Existence.
2. Send thoughts of peace and good will toward all beings—

transmitting these thoughts consciously toward the four points of the compass in turn: north, south, east and west.

3. Think of your own body as a temple which contains the Real Self, the Reality, which is infinite existence, infinite knowledge and infinite peace. (The Sanskrit words used to describe the nature of the Reality are *sat-chit-ananda.* The Reality does not have *sat* (existence), it *is* existence. It is also *chit,* consciousness; that is to say, it is all knowledge. It is also *ananda,* peace; the word I have already referred to, at the beginning of this chapter. *Ananda* is the peace of the spirit—in Christian language, "the peace of God which passeth all understanding." *Ananda* may also be translated as "bliss"; because absolute peace, independent of all change and circumstance, is the only genuine happiness.)

4. The Reality in yourself is the Reality within all other beings.

To sum up: this plan of meditation was a three-stage process. You sent your thoughts outward to the surrounding world, drew them inward upon yourself, then sent them outward again—but with a difference; for now you were no longer thinking of your fellow creatures as mere individuals but as temples containing the Reality. As mortal beings, you had offered them your good will; as the Eternal, you now offered them your reverence.

I have described all this in detail in order to illustrate an important point: these first instructions given me by the Swami had no reference to the cult of any personal God-figure or divine incarnation. The assumptions they contained—that the Reality exists and can be contacted and known—were nondualistic assumptions. Knowledge of the Reality, in this context, means unitive knowledge—i.e. the realization that you, essentially, *are* the Reality, always were the Reality, and always will be. Where, then, does the personal God-figure fit into this philosophy? Is there a place for him at all?

Yes, there is. The dualistic God—the God-who-is-other-than-I—is an aspect of the Reality but not other than the Reality. Within the world of phenomena—the world of apartness, of this and that, of we and you—the God-who-is-other-than-we is the greatest phenomenon of all. But, with the experience of unitive, nondualistic knowledge, the God-who-is-other-than-I merges into the God-who-is-myself. The divine phenomena are seen to be all aspects of the one central Reality.

Let me deal with one simple misunderstanding which troubled me, and may trouble my readers. To say "I am God" is at one and the same time the most blasphemous statement you could possibly make, and also the truest. It all depends on what you mean by "I." If you mean, "my ego is God, Christopher Isherwood is God," then you are blaspheming; if you mean "my essential Self is God," then you are speaking the truth. It follows from this that you can never become one with the God-who-is-other-than-you—for "God" in this sense is also a projection of the central Reality. If you struggle, through meditation, for unitive knowledge of, let us say, Christ, there are two obstacles between you and its realization. One of them is your own individuality; the other is the individuality of Christ himself. If union is achieved, both these individualities must disappear; otherwise, the Reality within you cannot merge with the Reality within Christ.

This concept must naturally seem shocking to anyone who has been raised with a purely dualistic attitude to religion. And yet, for the nondualist, the dualistic approach to God seems altogether appropriate and, in many cases, preferable. It is almost impossible for me, in my average unregenerate state, to believe that I am a temple which contains the Reality. All I know of myself is my ego, and that appears to be a pretty squalid temple containing nothing of any value. So it is natural for me to turn toward some other being, one who really acts and speaks and appears as though the Reality were within him. By making a cult of this being—by adoring him and trying to resemble him —I can gradually come to an awareness of the Reality within myself. There you have the whole virtue of the cult.

THE GROUP of which Swami Prabhavananda was the leader was called officially The Vedanta Society of Southern California—

a nonprofit religious corporation, established, in the words of its constitution, "to promote the study of the philosophy of Vedanta . . . . and to promote harmony between Eastern and Western thought, and recognition of the truth in all the great religions of the world." (Vedanta means the philosophy which is taught in the Vedas—the most ancient of the Hindu Scriptures. Thus one might say that Vedanta stands to Yoga in the relation of theory to practice. Vedanta teaches us the nature of God and the Universe. Yoga teaches us the ways in which union with God may be attained.)

WHEN you first entered the temple of the Vedanta Society, you might well be surprised by its plainness—especially if the curtains at the far end of it were drawn together. It was simply a lecture-room, tastefully decorated in light grey, with comfortable rows of seats facing a kind of pulpit on a platform. On the walls were photographs of Ramakrishna, his wife (usually called the Holy Mother), his chief disciples Vivekananda and Brahmananda, together with a picture of an image of the Buddha and of the alleged head of Christ on the Turin Shroud. There were no Hindu paintings or draperies or ornaments; nothing specifically Indian except for the Sanskrit word Om, which was carved on the pulpit. (Om is the word for God the Central Reality; it includes every deity, every aspect of the divine, but refers particularly to none. The word Om is chosen because it is thought to be the most comprehensive of all sounds, beginning back in the open throat and ending on the closed lips; and thus symbolizing God, the all-encompassing.)

Thus, when you first entered the temple, you didn't at all feel that you were caught in a religious spider's web. Being there didn't commit you to anything. You could sit down in a mood of objective curiosity and listen to one of the Swami's Sunday lectures on Vedanta philosophy. The audience was not required to participate in any act of worship, either before or after the lectures. Nor, if you were a Christian, did you need to leave your beliefs at home. The Swami always took it for granted that there would be many Christians among his hearers, and he constantly referred to Christ's teachings to illustrate the points he was making. In his eyes, Christ was one of the great spiritual teachers of mankind, to be spoken of with the deepest reverence. But this degree of recognition wouldn't, of course, have satisfied the orthodox Christian minister of any sect. For such a minister, the Swami was still a heathen—even if an enlightened one— because he didn't admit that Christ was the *only* teacher, the *only* doorway to the truth.

But the temple had another aspect. It really *was* a temple, and not merely the lecture-room of a philosophical society. When the curtains were drawn apart, you saw that there was a small windowless shrineroom beyond the platform on which the pulpit stood. Within this shrineroom, on a pedestal of two steps, stood the shrine itself. It had been made in India, of intricately carved, highly polished dark wood; four double corinthian pillars supporting a dome. This shrine was exposed to the full view of the audience during the Swami's lectures. Decked with garlands of flowers and lit by candles in glass candlesticks with sparkling pendants, it looked magically pretty; and no doubt the casual visitor to the temple, who saw it from the distance of his seat in the lecture hall, thought of it merely as a charming and picturesque focal point in the scheme of decoration. As a matter of fact, it was the focal point of the whole life of the Vedanta Society.

For the Society, as I gradually discovered, didn't only exist to propagate the study of Vedanta philosophy. That was only one half—the less important half—of its purpose. The major purpose of the Society was to encourage its members to lead lives in which the search for the Reality was a central preoccupation and a matter of daily private practice, not just public Sunday observance. Even the busiest of them were expected to find time every day for meditation. Some acutally had shrines in their own homes. Many were devotees of Ramakrishna as a divine incarnation; but Prabhavananda never insisted on this. If you preferred to meditate on Christ, or any other holy figure, or upon the impersonal God, then you were taught how to do so.

The Swami himself belonged to an order of Indian monks called the Ramakrishna Order. It had been founded by Vivekananda, one of Ramakrishna's two chief disciples; the other, Brahmananda, had been the first head of the Order and the guru (teacher) of Prabhavananda. So we in Hollywood might feel ourselves to be still very near to the fountainhead.

Under the dome of the shrine, a photograph of Ramakrishna occupied the central position. To the right of this was a photograph of Holy Mother; to the left were images of Buddha and Krishna and a Russian icon of Christ. Photographs of Brahmananda and Vivekananda stood on the lower level, together with images of some other Hindu deities. Meditation-periods, accompanied by ritual worship, were held in the shrineroom three times a day by the Swami and those members of the group who wished to take part in them. Though the Swami taught all his pupils to meditate, he never said that they must take part, directly or indirectly, in the ritual worship. Ritual worship and indeed the whole cult of a divine personality, formed, according to his teaching, only one of the several ways, the yogas, to knowledge of the Reality. The Swami told us that there was actually one monastery of the Ramakrishna Order—Mayavati in the Himalayas—at which there was no shrine and no ritual worship, in order that the monks might accustom themselves to meditating without these adjuncts.

It didn't take much experience of meditation in the shrineroom—which I now visited whenever I had time—to bring home to me one self-evident fact: that a spiritual atmosphere—or indeed any other kind of an atmosphere—can be deliberately created. In this case, the atmosphere of the shrineroom was extraordinarily calming, and yet *alive*. When you came into it, with your head full of the anxieties and preoccupations of the outside world, you found yourself relaxing almost at once: but not—as would have happened in any ordinary quiet place—

into sleep. One of my friends said that it was like being in a wood; and this seemed to me a very apt description. Just as, in a wood, you can become aware that the trees are alive all around you, so I sometimes felt as if the shrineroom were filled with consciousness—the consciousness of all those who were meditating and had meditated in it.

But the shrine was something more than this. It was more than a kind of meditation-bank, into which we had made deposits and which now paid interest. It was also a holy place, a living presence. Within the shrine were relics of Ramakrishna, Holy Mother and their disciples. The Hindus believe—as the Catholics believe—that such relics give forth power; that they generate spiritual radiations which can actually affect the lives of those who are exposed to them. The Swami believed that, by virtue of the relics, Ramakrishna and the others were present within the shrine in a special sense; and that it was therefore absolutely necessary that the ritual worship should be performed before it every day.

MY reactions to the temple and what it stood for can probably be imagined—both pro and con. (I have since found them to be the usual reactions of anyone who comes into contact with the Vedanta Society for the first time—always providing that he or she hasn't had previous dealings with Theosophy or some other system of metaphysics; in which case a different response-pattern is set up.) On the con side, I was of course powerfully repelled by the specifically Indian aspects of the Ramakrishna cult. Why did the rituals in the shrine have to be Hindu rituals? Why did several of the women devotees like to wear saris in the shrineroom? Why were the prayers in Sanskrit? Why did we so often have curry at meals?

I think these objections were rooted in a twofold prejudice. Whether I liked it or not, I had been brought up in the Christian tradition; anything outside that tradition repelled me as being unnecessarily alien. Also, as a member, whether I liked it or not, of the British upper class, I had somewhere deep inside me a built-in contempt for the culture of "native," "subject" races. If my subconscious had been allowed to speak out clearly, it would have said: "I quite admit that you have the truth, but does it have to come to me wearing a turban? Can't I be an Anglo-Saxon Vedantist?" In fact, it would have talked like Naaman the leper in the Bible story. Naaman had the greatest respect for Elisha. He believed that Elisha could cure him of his leprosy. But he hated to be told to wash himself in the river Jordan. "Are not Abana and Pharpar, rivers of Damascus, better than all the waters of Israel?" Aren't the Rhine and the Hudson better than the Ganges?

But, in my pro mood, I was easily able to answer these objections. In the first place, if you have made up your mind to worship God in a particular form, then obviously you have to start with the externals. You have to recognize the fact that Ramakrishna was an Indian and that Christ was a Jew (a fact, incidentally, which many Christians try hard to forget). Lack of documentations permits the Christian to imagine Christ's physical appearance more or less as he likes. Of Ramakrishna we have photographs.

Having pictured the man, you next have to picture his surroundings; the place he lived in, the clothes he wore, the food he ate, the kind of people and events which would fill his exterior everyday life. It is most important to do this, because you then have to try to fit yourself into the scene; to approach Ramakrishna in his own proper setting, asking yourself, "Should *I* have recognized him, then, for what he really was?"

When you think of the problem in this way, it is easy to see the value of these Indian accessories; to see why you should perform the same rituals which Ramakrishna himself used to perform, as a young priest; why you should say prayers and chant chants in the language that he spoke; why, while you are trying to meditate upon him, you should wear the chadars or saris which are native to his country; why, even, you should eat the food that he ate.

And so the seesaw of reactions goes back and forth. The devotee does not want to turn himself into a kind of synthetic Hindu—no; that would be ridiculous and anyhow impossible. But he does want to get as close to the personality of Ramakrishna as he can; even on the external level. So the Indian-ness alternately repels and attracts him. That, at least, was my own experience. Luckily for me and for the many others who felt as I did, Swami Prabhavananda had a deeply sympathetic and often humorous understanding of our difficulty. Indeed, it was this understanding which set the whole tone of life in the small household which was then the nucleus of the Vedanta Society.

And now I should say something about the Society itself: how and why it started.

IN 1886, immediately after Ramakrishna's death in Calcutta, the inner ring of disciples, led by Vivekananda and Brahmananda, bound themselves together by taking *sannyas,* the final monastic vow. They did not, however, immediately form an official monastic order.

In 1893, Vivekananda came to America, to attend a Parliament of Religions which was being held as part of the Columbian Exposition in Chicago. Although Vivekananda was unknown and was not an official delegate—his traveling expenses had been scraped together with great difficulty—his success as a speaker was enormous. At the end of the Parliament's session, he was asked to visit many cities in the States and to found centers in which the teaching of Vedanta could be continued.

(It is to be noted that Vivekananda appeared primarily as a teacher of Vedanta, not a gospeler of Ramakrishna, his Master. "If I had preached the personality of Ramakrishna," he used to remark later, "I might have converted half the world: but that kind of conversion is short-lived. So instead I preached Ramakrishna's principles. If people accept the principles they will eventually accept the personality.")

In 1897, after Vivekananda's return to India, he and his brother monks conferred together and put the activities of the Ramakrishna Order on an organized basis. First, a Mission was founded; then, two years later, a Math (monastery). The headquarters of both Math and Mission are at Belur, just outside Calcutta; branch centers have gradually been opened all over India. The Mission is primarily active in social work, running schools and hospitals and administering famine or epidemic relief projects; the Math is primarily active in the training of monks and in ritual worship. But the two are not really separate entities, except for the convenience of planning and the allotment of funds. Swamis of the Order keep exchanging one way of life for the other: spending some time in meditation and solitude, then taking on administrative duties at one of the Mission centers.

In 1899, Vivekananda came back to the United States. This time, he was chiefly occupied in forming centers and training devotees. He arranged for swamis of the Ramakrishna Order to come over from India and take charge of these centers.

In the early part of 1900, during this visit, Vivekananda spent six weeks at the house of three sisters who lived in Pasadena, California. One of these was Mrs. Carrie Mead Wyckoff, a widow. Vivekananda returned to India and died in 1902, but Mrs. Wyckoff never lost touch with the Ramakrishna Order. She met two other direct disciples of Ramakrishna, Swamis Turiyananda and Trigunatita, both of whom came to America to supervise the San Francisco Vedanta center. Swami Trigunatita gave her a Sanskrit name-in-religion; this was a usual practice among the devotees of the Order. He called her Sister Lalita (Lalita was one of the handmaidens of Krishna), and it was as "Sister" that she was always known at the time when I met her.

In 1928, Sister met Swami Prabhavananda. He had been sent to the States five years previously, as assistant to Swami Prakashananda who was then the head of the San Francisco Center. Later he had founded a Vedanta Society in Portland, Oregon, at the request of some devotees of Ramakrishna who were living there.

In 1929, Sister invited Prabhavananda to come down to Los
Angeles, and she put her modest house and income at the dis-
posal of the future Vedanta Society of Southern California. At
first, it was a very small Society indeed. An Englishwoman
whom they called Amiya came to keep house for the elderly lady
and the youthful monk; after a while, they were joined by two or
three others. The Swami's lectures were given in the living room,
and it was quite big enough to hold his tiny audience. Financial-
ly speaking, they lived from week to week. The Swami often did
the cooking. Going to the movies was an occasional and special
treat. Nevertheless, they seem to have had a great deal of fun.

Then, around 1936, the congregation began to expand con-
siderably. Prabhavananda became locally well known as a speaker
and respected as an individual. It was now only rarely that anyone would telephone to ask if the Swami would draw up a horo-
scope or give a public performance of his yoga powers. In fact,
word had got around that this *wasn't* a Swami in the usual
California sense. And now enough money was donated to build
a temple. Sister's house had already been enlarged to include a
shrineroom, but this was much too small; and the living room
was no longer big enough for the lectures. Finding a site for the
temple presented no problem; for there was room in Sister's
garden. So the work went ahead; and the temple was completed
and dedicated in July 1938, about a year before I first set eyes on it.

But although the Society was steadily growing—although
quite a lot of people came to hear Swami speak on Sundays, and
even more to hear Gerald Heard, who sometimes took his place
—the group in Sister's house was still very much a family. "The
Lord's Family," the Swami called it; and you really did feel,
even as an outside visitor, that Ramakrishna was established in
that household, that he presided over it in a curiously intimate,
domestic manner. There was no dividing-line between the activities of the temple and the daily life of the group. Cooking and
even eating the lunch was actually all part of the ritual worship,
since a portion of what you were going to eat was first offered to
the Lord during the worship in the shrineroom and then brought

back and mixed in with the rest of the food, thus consecrating the entire meal and making it sacramental. And, as the inevitable result of all this going and coming between shrine and kitchen, the women of the household had lost any sense of "sacred" and "profane." They carried their jokes back and forth between the Eternal and the temporal; cooking-disasters and mistakes in the ritual were discussed at table in exactly the same tone of voice and with the same amount of amusement. Yes, there were times when all this Hinduism seemed sticky and theatrical and cloyingly sentimental. But it certainly brought Ramakrishna close to you—it was almost shamelessly cozy—and oh, I used to think to myself, oh, my goodness, what a relief from the reverent stuffiness of the Sunday religion I had been brought up in!

In the late autumn of 1940, when I had been coming to the Vedanta Society for about fifteen months, Prabhavananda decided to initiate me. The ceremony of initiation is standard Hindu practice: it consists, essentially, in the giving of a mantra by the guru to his disciple. The word *mantra* cannot be exactly translated into English, though the idea it expresses is not foreign to the Christian tradition. The mantra consists of several holy names, which the disciple is to repeat and meditate upon, for the rest of his life. It is regarded as very sacred and very private. You must never tell your mantra to any other human being. The act of repeating it is called *japa*. Because one usually resolves to make a certain fixed amount of japa every day, it is convenient to use a rosary. The rosary serves to measure the japa—one bead to each repetition of the mantra—so that you are not distracted by having to count.

The ceremony of initiation was necessarily a simple one, since it had to be repeated several times. Prabhavananda would usually initiate four or five people on the same day. The day chosen would be one of our special festivals: this one was the birthday of the Holy Mother.

The initiation took place before breakfast, right after the first of the day's three meditation periods. Before going into the

temple, I was provided by one of the women of the family with a
small tray on which were arranged the flowers I was to offer:
two red roses, a white rose and a large daisy. The Swami was
waiting for me inside the shrine; its curtains had been drawn for
privacy. First, he told me to offer the flowers; to the photographs of Ramakrishna and Holy Mother, to the icon of Christ,
and to himself—because the guru must always receive at least a
token of an initiation-gift. Next, he taught me my mantra, making me repeat it several times until I was quite sure of it. Next, he
gave me a rosary and showed me how to use it. (The Hindu
rosaries are made of small dried seeds which come from the East
Indian islands, strung on a silk thread. There are 108 beads, plus
a lead-bead with a tassel attached to it. When you are "telling"
the beads, you never make a complete rotation because, when
you come to the tassel-bead, you reverse the rosary and start it
the other way around. The tassel-bead is said to represent the
Guru. Out of the hundred and eight repetitions of the mantra
which make up one rotation, one hundred are said to be for your
own devotions and the other eight are made on behalf of the rest
of mankind. These latter represent a labor of love, and are therefore not counted; so, for the purposes of reckoning how much
japa you intend to make daily, you count each rotation of the
rosary as one hundred only. I suppose the average amount of
japa made by an energetic devotee would be between five and
ten thousand a day.)

With my initiation, I entered into a kind of relationship
which will seem hopelessly strange or perhaps quite incompre-
hensible to many of my readers. I mean the relationship between
guru and disciple. It is not that I am trying to sound mysteriously
impressive or that I am laying claim to any great mystical experience. Indeed, I do not pretend to understand much about this
relationship myself.

In India, the guru-disciple relationship is regarded as being
of the greatest possible importance. It is essential to find yourself
a guru, because your guru is the nearest link in a chain which

connects you with one of the great spiritual teachers and hence with direct knowledge of God. This chain is a spiritual life line to all who can grasp hold of it. It is in this sense that the Hindu scriptures declare: "The Guru is God."

Having found your guru, you must now persuade him to initiate you; for it is only with initiation that the relationship can properly be said to have begun. But the guru may well hesitate before agreeing to this, because, in accepting a new disciple, he is taking on yet another tremendous responsibility. According to Hindu belief, the tie between guru and disciple can never be broken, either in this world or any other. It survives death, separation, estrangement and even downright betrayal. In other words, there would be no way for a Christ to disown a Judas.

The mantra is the guru's greatest gift to his disciple. It is, as it were, the essence of his teaching and of himself. By virtue of the mantra, the guru is present with the disciple at all times, no matter how far they may be apart. And just as the guru is the link in a physical chain of teachers, so the mantra is a link in a spiritual chain which corresponds to it.

What is more, the mantra always contains one or more "seed-words," as they are called. (The chief of these is the word *Om,* which I have already referred to.) These seed-words are regarded by the Hindus as being infinitely more than just words. They actually contain God's presence. Here, at least, is a concept which should not seem strange to Western minds. Every Christian knows how the Gospel according to John begins: "In the beginning was the Word, and the Word was with God, and the Word was God." What very, very few Christians know is that they could find in the Rig Veda, one of the Hindu scriptures which dates from many centuries earlier, a verse: "In the beginning was Brahman, with whom was the Word; and the Word was truly the supreme Brahman" (i.e. the transcendent Reality). Seed-words are no longer employed by Christians, it is true. But the Catholics do use rosaries and make what corresponds to japa. "Hail Mary" is a form of mantra. And, in the teachings of the

Greek Orthodox Church, we find that a prayer of constant repetition is recommended, the prayer in this case being "Lord Jesus Christ, have mercy on me."

As to the efficacy of such a prayer, it is only necessary to tell the reader to try it. No amount of mockery, or argument, will ever prove anything to him, either way. It is like the symbolic pump handle in Tolstoy's *A Confession*. If you move it up and down, you may get water. If you deny that it *is* a pump handle and refuse even to try it, then you most certainly never will.

At the Vedanta Society, we had always before us the example of a guru-disciple relationship which really generated power. I have said that Swami Prabhavananda was a disciple of Brahmananda. Brahmananda had died in 1922, and Prabhavananda had not even seen so very much of his guru while he was alive; for Brahmananda had many duties as head of the Order and had had to travel constantly from one monastery to another. And yet Brahmananda had been, and still was, the one dominant figure in Prabhavananda's life. He told us with absolute sincerity that he believed Brahmananda had all of us in his charge; that Brahmananda was personally directing the development of our Society. Whatever any of us might think of these statements, we couldn't doubt that the Swami not only meant them but also— which was far more impressive—led his own life *as if* they were true. He really did have the air of a second-in-command, and this attitude gave him a fundamental lack of vanity. I soon came to realize this and to respect it.

This lack of vanity was demonstrated by Swami's firm refusal to try to make an impression on those who met him. For example, quite a number of people were shocked by his chain-smoking of cigarettes. Horrors—you thought at first—an addiction! Later, you began to ask yourself if you would really have preferred to have a guru without weaknesses. How could one love, or even admire, such a creature? (As a matter of fact, many years later, Prabhavananda suddenly and completely gave up smoking—not on moral grounds but because the doctor told him to.)

The question may well be asked: what if the guru I find for myself is a bad man, a hypocrite, a pretender? The answer to this seems to be: if you pick the wrong guru, you will only have yourself to blame. This may sound rather heartless; but it is impossible, on the other hand, not to agree that the many gullible rich women of this country who make possible the existence of fake religions are quite as guilty as the false prophets who run them. The Hindu idea is that you should subject your prospective guru to every kind of test, until you are entirely convinced of his honesty. Then, and only then, should you submit your will to him and obey him absolutely. At the same time, it may be said as a consolation to the unwise that a bad guru is not a dead loss. The Catholics believe that the sacraments administered by a morally bad priest are still valid. The Hindus believe that a mantra given by a morally bad swami is still valid. The chain of spiritual power remains unbroken.

Finally there comes the question: how will I set about finding a guru? To this the Hindus answer: when you really need a guru, you will find one. This is one of the many statements about religious matters which I must—in Gerald Heard's phrase—"put into my suspense account." I don't say I don't believe it; but, in my present stage of ignorance, I have no way of finding out if it is true. That it has been true in my own case is evident. That it is true universally, I would like to believe—if only because the alternative seems to be a Calvinistic smugness. You are never in deadlier danger than when you believe you have been individually "chosen" and "saved."

3.

As the war went on, and the fighting spread over larger and larger areas of the world, and as it became increasingly probable that the United States would become directly involved in it before long, I began to feel that I must "do something." This urge—which was then being experienced by hundreds of thousands of others, all over the country—was caused by the terrible psychic restlessness which a war-situation generates. It is experienced as guilt: you feel you ought to be sharing the sufferings of the combatants, you ought to be, somehow, "in it." While you are in this state of guilt-restlessness, you are apt to overlook two facts: that people have been suffering somewhere on this earth in various unadvertised and uninteresting ways, ever since you were born, and that you have never let it spoil your appetite or your sleep; that the "something" which it now seems worthwhile for you to be doing is quite probably much less constructive and socially valuable than the work you are doing at present —work which you are now rejecting as inappropriate to the war-situation.

Looking back on those years, I feel that I should have been much better employed staying close to the Vedanta Society and learning more of what it had to teach, so that I could be instrumental in passing that teaching on to others at a time when there was a desperate need of it. But no—I was too restless. So I went east to Pennsylvania and worked at a Quaker hostel for war-refugees from Europe. Nearly all of these refugees were German or Austrian. I spoke German well enough to be able to give them English lessons and thus prepare them to take jobs in America; so I was at least able to make myself useful, even if this wasn't the kind of work for which I was really fitted.

But the time I spent with the Friends—from October 1941 to July 1942—was most valuable, as far as I was concerned. They gave me far more, indeed, than I was able to give them. They gave me, among other things, a new viewpoint from which to assess my experiences of Vedanta. This is no place in which to write all that I then felt and now still feel about the Friends and their way of life. They are, to my mind, the most admirable and the most dedicated of all Christian sects—though I must add that they are probably able to preserve many of their virtues only at the price of being such a small and relatively uninfluential group. There are less than 80,000 Quakers in the U.S.A.

What is relevant to my present subject is this: The Society of Friends is, as far as I am aware, the Christian sect which comes closest to agreement with the teachings of Vedanta. The Friends believe that a religious life can only be lived by constantly meditating upon and recollecting the presence of an "Inner Light" within the heart. This Inner Light is what the Hindu would call the Atman, the Reality within the individual. Like the Atman, the Inner Light is impersonal; though it may in practice be regarded by nearly all Quakers as the light of Christ's teaching. In practice, no doubt, all Quakers are Christians. But, theoretically, you don't have to be a Christian to be a Quaker. The Inner Light might just as well be regarded as proceeding from Ramakrishna.

On the spiritual level, the Society of Friends is not a church. It does not have a creed. It issues no dogmas. It has no corporate belief—except for the simple, basic belief that the Inner Light exists and that it may be appealed to for guidance. Each Friend seeks this guidance for himself. The Society is literally a society. It is organized only for social and administrative purposes.

I suppose that, if I hadn't already met Prabhavananda, I might have become a Quaker. There was nothing in the Quaker way of life with which I couldn't agree, in theory at least. In practice, I might have have found the Friends' attitude to the Arts somewhat philistine. But there were many exceptions to this general rule, and it would have been up to me to join with them and do something to make the majority more liberal.

In any case, I wasn't much interested at that time in the failure of Friends to enjoy the subtleties of T. S. Eliot, modern painting, or the Ballet; what mattered to me was their stand for pacifism. The Society did not, of course, prescribe a uniform response to this problem; to have done so would have been contrary to its spirit. Some young Quakers even accepted combat service in the armed forces. But the great majority were pacifists of some sort—ranging all the way from those who were willing to work in the medical corps to those who refused even to register for the draft (holding this action to be a tacit approval of the military machine) and were therefore sent to prison.

As for myself, having already taken out my first citizenship papers and being subject to the U.S. draft, I had decided to take the legal middle course which the draft-law provided: non-combatant civilian public service, in a forestry-camp. In the spring of 1942, registration began for the higher age group to which I belonged, and I registered as a conscientious objector. Since I did this in a neighborhood where Quakers were numerous and respected, I was subjected to none of the bullying which C.O.'s had to suffer in many other parts of the country. I got my 4-E classification immediately. Soon after this, I went back to California. The hostel at which I had been working was being disbanded, because it was easy to find employment for nearly all of our refugees now that labor was getting scarcer and scarcer, owing to the war-situation. Also, you were allowed to choose the camp you would serve in, and I wanted to be in one of the camps in California, where there were several of my friends.

However, things turned out otherwise. The draft-authorities discovered that older men were often more trouble to the armed forces than they were worth; they got sick and you had to pension them. So the age limit was lowered again, and I was no longer liable for service. I found myself with nothing to do.

I suppose I would soon have become involved in some other voluntary project of the Friends Service Committee if Swami Prabhavananda hadn't, at this moment, made the suggestion that I should come up to stay at the Vedanta Center and work with him on a translation of the Bhagavad-Gita.

THE GITA, (its full title means *The Blessed Lord's Song*) is often referred to as "the Gospel of Hinduism," because it contains the teachings of Krishna, who may be said to be the Christ of India. (Lest this remark should sound provincial, I hasten to add that Christ, the later comer, might with more justice be called the Krishna of Palestine. There are, indeed, several striking parallel incidents in the recorded lives of these two avatars.) In any case, the Gita is undoubtedly the most frequently read and quoted of the Hindu religious classics. Its teachings were often on the lips of Ramakrishna. It was the daily inspiration of Gandhi. It has influenced the spiritual, cultural and even the political life of India throughout the centuries, and continues to do so.

The Gita is a most unusual kind of composition, for it has been designed to fit into the middle of another literary work, the Mahabharata. But while the Gita is a religious-philosophical poem, the Mahabharata is an epic—the longest, it is said, in all literature. It consists of about one hundred thousand verses. Its central theme is the story of the descendants of King Bharata (*Maha* means great) and of ancient India, where the Bharatas lived and ruled.

For the purposes of this explanation, it is only necessary to say that Arjuna, the warrior-hero of the story, is about to lead his men in a civil war against the forces of his wicked foster brother Duryodhana, who has tricked him and his own brothers out of their inherited kingdom. The neighbors have been drawn into this quarrel, so that now every chieftain in India has taken sides.

Both sides have appealed to Krishna—who at that time was living on earth in human form—for his help. To both, Krishna has offered the same choice: "Either you can have my kinsmen the Vrishnis as your allies in the war, or you can have me alone; but I shall simply be present without taking any part in the fighting." Duryodhana, being a mere opportunist, naturally chooses the physical help of the Vrishnis. Arjuna prefers the moral and spiritual support of his beloved friend Krishna, and takes him for his personal charioteer.

Thus far the Mahabharata. Now the Gita takes up the narrative and tells how, just before the battle is to begin, Arjuna asks Krishna to drive him out into the no-man's-land between the two armies. He wants to see the men he is going to fight against. Krishna does as he is asked and Arjuna is shocked—for now he becomes aware that the enemy ranks are filled with his kinsfolk and friends. He does not want to kill these men. He exclaims in desperation that he would rather lose the battle and be killed himself. He will not fight. Krishna, however, rejects this attitude and a long philosophical dialogue follows—of which more in a moment. The upshot of it is that Arjuna decides that he was wrong. He *will* fight, after all. He has complete confidence in Krishna's judgment. His mind stands firm. His doubts are answered.

At this point, the Gita ends. But here we can turn back to the Mahabharata and continue the story without a break, reading how the battle was then fought on the plain of Kurukshetra and lasted eighteen days, ending with the death of Duryodhana and the complete victory of Arjuna and his brothers. As I said above, the Gita fits perfectly into the Mahabharata narrative; but it was not originally part of it. Most scholars believe that it was composed independently, sometime between the fifth and second centuries B.C.

During the year and a half—approximately from the late summer of 1942 to the beginning of 1944—that I worked with Swami Prabhavananda on the Gita translation, I discussed its philosophy with many different people. However little or much they knew about it, I found that they were almost all agreed on one point: that it sanctioned War. Some found satisfaction in this, others deplored it; but all, I think, were puzzled. Educated in the Christian tradition, they were accustomed to a Gospel which is uncompromisingly pacifist. The majority of them set aside the teachings of the Gospel, it is true—by the worst of luck, it always seems to happen that this particular war you are fighting is exceptionally necessary and just!—but they were rather shocked when one of their spiritual superiors appeared to be approving the use of military force in general. They themselves, mere humans struggling in the everyday world, might be driven to kill each other; but they wanted Krishna, like Jesus, to stand for a higher ideal.

As a pacifist, I naturally regarded this as a question of major importance. If the Gita really did unconditionally sanction war, then I must reject it as I had long ago rejected the Old Testament. So it was urgently necessary for me to figure out what the Gita *did* mean. What follows is the interpretation which I finally arrived at, under Prabhavananda's guidance. It satisfied my doubts at the time, and it still seems quite valid to me. So I now offer it to any perplexed pacifists who may be among my readers.

First of all, I must say that an objection such as mine was of course not unusual. Gandhi, like many others no doubt, solved it by deciding that the Gita must be regarded as an allegory: Arjuna is the individual soul when it is under the influence of its higher impulses; Krishna is the Atman, the indwelling Godhead; Arjuna's enemies are the soul's evil tendencies, and so forth.

Again, there are those who try to mitigate what they feel to be the Gita's militaristic teaching by pointing out that the conditions under which the battle of Kurukshetra (or any historical battle of that era) was fought were greatly different from those of modern warfare. Kurukshetra was a kind of tournament, governed by all the elaborate and relatively humane rules of classical Indian chivalry. A soldier mounted upon an elephant was not allowed to attack a foot soldier. No man might be struck or shot at while running away. No man might be killed after he had lost his weapons. And the Mahabharata tells us that the opposing armies stopped fighting every day at sunset, and even visited each other and fraternized during the night.

This second interpretation of the Gita seems to me irrelevant. Tournament or no tournament, people lost their lives at Kurukshetra in great numbers. And if the Sixth Commandment means anything at all, it means that thou shalt not kill even one single human being, either with a spear or a hydrogen bomb. As for the first interpretation, I must say, despite my most sincere respect for Gandhi, that it does not satisfy me. This question is too serious to be sidestepped in such a manner; and an allegory, however beautiful or ingenious, offers little or no spiritual support in a crisis. If the Gita has any validity, its message must hold good for our own day and age.

To understand the Gita, we must first consider what it is and what it is not. We must consider its setting. When Jesus preached the Sermon on the Mount, he was far from the city and his enemies, in the heart of the countryside. Moreover, he was speaking in general terms, without reference to any immediate crisis or personal problem. It is true that, at a moment of acute danger, in the Garden of Gethsemane, he remained true to his pacifist principles and told Peter to sheathe the sword he had drawn to save his Master from arrest; but it must be remembered that Peter was a dedicated disciple, whom Jesus was training for a missionary life. For him there could be no compromise. He had to be reminded constantly of the highest ideal, that of non-violence.

In the Gita story, the situation is quite different: Krishna and Arjuna are on a battlefield; Arjuna is a warrior by birth and profession. He belongs to the caste of the Kshatriyas, whose duty it is to be administrators in peacetime and leaders in war. His ideals of conduct are in most respects those of a mediaeval Christian knight.

Arjuna's problem is an immediate one. He has to make up his mind in this very hour, to fight or not to fight. The problem relates to him *as he is at that moment;* it has nothing to do with any change in his philosophy and ideals which may occur in the future.

The fact that Krishna's teaching in the Gita is inspired by a particular problem of a particular individual at one particular moment is, I believe, a cause of misunderstanding to many readers. We all tend to remember most clearly how a book begins, because we read the opening chapters while our interest is fresh. But the opening chapters deal with Arjuna's case only. Later on,

Krishna passes from the particular to the general, and teaches the same truths which were afterwards taught by the Buddha and by Jesus. Too late! The superficial reader has got nothing from the Gita but his first impression. Remembering only Arjuna and the battle, he says to himself: Krishna tells us to fight.

Even Arjuna himself questions his motives in shrinking from the battle. After saying, of some of his kinsmen who are among the enemy, "If we kill them, none of us will wish to live," he appeals to Krishna: "Is this real compassion that I feel, or only a delusion? My mind gropes about in darkness. I cannot see where my duty lies."

In answering and teaching Arjuna, Krishna employs two sets of values, relative and absolute. He speaks with two voices. This duality is inherent in his own nature; he is Arjuna's friend and fellow mortal, and he is God. Ramakrishna used to explain that one who knows God is compelled to revert temporarily to a state of ego-consciousness in order to teach others. If the Atman is experienced, then the personality is seen to be a mere mask; the notion that you are "yourself" rather than somebody else becomes meaningless. Seeing God inside means also seeing God outside and everywhere; and how can God teach God? In order to take the measure of Arjuna's ignorance and to answer his doubts, Krishna has to view them from the standpoint of relativity. He must cease for a moment to see Arjuna—and all other men—as a dwelling place of the Atman, and regard him instead as a specific individual whose name is Arjuna, the third son of Pandu and Kunti and the general in command of this army which is about to fight this battle.

But the voice of Krishna's assumed teacher-ego consciousness is often interrupted while another voice speaks through his body; the voice of God. Arjuna does not doubt the genuineness of this voice; he is prepared to believe that Krishna is a divine incarnation. Nevertheless, being only human, he asks for absolute proof; and Krishna supplies this by granting a beautiful but appalling vision of himself as the Lord of the Universe. And now Arjuna realizes just how weak and partial his previous faith had been—necessarily so, perhaps, since man cannot bear conscious companionship with God. He now asks Krishna's pardon:

> Carelessly I called you "Krishna" and "my comrade,"
> Took undying God for friend and fellow-mortal,
> Overbold with love, unconscious of your greatness.

Krishna is quick to reassure Arjuna, by speaking to him again as human to human. Indeed, he tells Arjuna: "You are the friend I chose and love." And Arjuna, reassured, slips back into acceptance of their personal relationship—which is what Krishna evidently wishes. We may infer a similar relationship between Jesus and his disciples after their vision of his transfiguration.

Here are examples of Krishna's two voices:

The Teacher: "Now I will tell you briefly about the nature of him who is called The Deathless by those seers who truly understand the Vedas."

God: "Know only that I exist, and that one atom of myself sustains the universe."

The difference in the tone of these two statements makes one gasp. Yet both were uttered by the same mouth and both—such is the inadequacy of language—employ the same word "I." Throughout the Gita, the teacher-voice and the God-voice of Krishna succeed each other frequently and without warning. No wonder so many readers become confused and explain that their teaching is self-contradictory! We have to keep the distinction clearly in mind when we analyze Krishna's reply to Arjuna's problem.

Krishna begins by dealing with Arjuna's feelings of revulsion, on general grounds. Arjuna shrinks from the act of killing. Krishna reminds him that, in the absolute sense, there is no such act. The Atman, the indwelling Godhead, is the only reality. This body is simply an appearance, the manifestation of a phase of being; its birth, life and death are alike illusory. In the absolute sense, all talk of killing or being killed is meaningless:

> Some say this Atman
> Is slain, and others
> Call it the slayer:
> They know nothing.
> How can it slay
> Or who shall slay it?

And, in a later passage, speaking as God the creator, sustainer and dissolver of all things, he says: "All these hosts must die; strike, stay your hand—no matter. Seem to slay. By me these men are slain already."

This is all very well and very true, no doubt. But it is not individually true for Arjuna, because he is not yet in a state of God-consciousness; he still thinks of himself as Arjuna, the warrior. So now Krishna uses his other voice and talks to Arjuna in the language he can best understand, the language of his own moral values:

"Even if you consider this from the standpoint of your own caste-duty, you ought not to hestitate; for, to a warrior, there is nothing nobler than a righteous war . . . . But if you refuse to fight this righteous war, you will be turning aside from your duty. You will be a sinner, and disgraced. People will speak ill of you throughout the ages."

For Arjuna, as a member of the warrior caste, the fighting of this battle in defense of his family and property is "righteous." It is his caste-duty. In the Gita, we find the caste-system presented as a kind of natural order. There are four main castes; the Brahmins, the Kshatriyas, the Vaishyas and the Sudras—priests, warriors, merchants and servants. In the last chapter of the Gita, the duties of the four castes are described. Since the four caste-types are being considered psychologically rather than sociologically, their names are here translated somewhat differently:

> Seer and leader,
> Provider and server:

Each has the duty
Ordained by his nature . . .

The seer's duty,
Ordained by his nature,
Is to be tranquil
In mind and in spirit
Self-controlled,
Austere and stainless,
Upright, forbearing;
To follow wisdom,
To know the Atman,
Firm of faith
In the truth that is Brahman.

The leader's duty,
Ordained by his nature,
Is to be bold,
Unflinching and fearless,
Subtle of skill
And open-handed
Great-hearted in battle,
A resolute ruler.

Others are born
To the tasks of providing:
These are the traders,
The cultivators,
The breeders of cattle.

To work for all men,
Such is the duty
Ordained for the servers:
This is their nature.

All mankind
Is born for perfection
And each shall attain it,
Will he but follow
His nature's duty.

Much has been said about the evils of the caste-system as a social structure; and these criticisms are justified, no doubt, with reference to our own age, into which the mere skeleton has been handed down, bereft of its life breath. But if we think of the castes as psychological categories rather than as social prison cells, we shall be much nearer to understanding what the Gita has to teach about them. It is perfectly obvious that Nature makes its own castes: seers, leaders, providers and servers are to be found among the members of any generation, anywhere on earth. All that the State can do about these basic types is to encourage or discourage the development of some or all of them; but in any case the types will continue to be born.

And whether the State likes it or not, each psychophysical type—and, indeed, each separate individual—has the peculiar ethics and responsibilities which are dictated by its own nature. These constitute what is called in Sanskrit its *dharma,* its "nature's duty." And it is only by following the line of this personal duty that one can grow in spirit. A man must go forward from where he stands. He cannot jump to the Absolute; he must evolve toward it. He cannot arbitrarily assume the duties which belong to another type. If he does so, his whole scale of values will be distorted, his conscience will no longer be able to direct him and he will stray into pride or doubt or mental confusion. "Prefer to die doing your own duty," Krishna tells Arjuna: "The duty of another will bring you into great spiritual danger."

By following his nature's duty, each one of us can attain spiritual perfection; that is Krishna's message. Seven of the saints of southern India were below the lowest caste, Untouchables. Ramakrishna was a Brahmin but he chose disciples from all of the four castes. And likewise among the saints of Christian Europe we find peasants and servants, merchants, soldiers, scholars, doctors, kings and popes.

Not only is it Arjuna's duty to fight, it is also his *karma.* The Sanskrit word karma has a primary and a secondary meaning. A karma is a mental or physical act. It is also the consequences of that act; good, bad or mixed. Since all Hindu and Buddhist philosophy presupposes a belief in the process of reincarnation, this act may have been performed in some previous life and yet continue to work out its consequences in this one. The Law of Karma is the natural law by which our present condition is simply the product of our past thoughts and actions, and by which we are always currently engaged in creating our own future.

So Arjuna is no longer a free agent. The act of war is upon him; it has evolved out of his previous actions. He can no longer choose. Krishna reminds him of this: "If, in your vanity, you say 'I will not fight,' your resolve is vain. Your own nature will drive you to the act." At any given moment in time, we are what we are; and our actions express that condition. We cannot run away from our actions because we carry the condition with us. On the highest mountain, in the darkest cave, we must turn at last and accept the consequences of being ourselves. Only through this acceptance can we begin to evolve further. We may choose the battleground. We cannot permanently avoid the battle.

But though the Law of Karma compels Arjuna to fight—or refrain from fighting out of mere cowardice, which is morally just as bad—he is still free to make his choice between two ways of performing the action. The right and the wrong performance of action is one of the principal themes of the Gita; Krishna introduces it early in the dialogue, immediately after he has reminded Arjuna of his caste-duty. What he now teaches applies not only to Arjuna but to all men at all times in their varying predicaments: "You have the right to work, but for the work's sake only. You have no right to the fruits of work . . . . Perform every action with your heart fixed on the Supreme Lord. Renounce all attachment to the fruits . . . . To unite the heart with Brahman and then to act: that is the secret of non-attached work. In the calm of self-surrender, the seers renounce the fruits of their actions, and so reach enlightenment. Then they are free from the bondage of rebirth, and pass to that state which is beyond all evil."

Ramakrishna was fond of saying that you could get the

essential message of the Gita by repeating the word several times. "Gita, Gita, Gita," you begin, but then you find yourself saying "ta-Gi, ta-Gi, ta-Gi." *Tagi* means one who has renounced everything for God.

But both Krishna and Ramakrishna made it clear that genuine renunciation is primarily a mental act. For the vast majority of us, it does not involve actually giving up our material possessions and worldly responsibilities. This is where the question has to be asked: what does my dharma demand of me? For the few, there is the vocation to a monastic life; for the many there is the life of the householder. For both, the mental act of renunciation is all-important. If you "renounce" action physically but not mentally, you are simply being lazy. If you break off relationships and give up belongings for the sake of playing the saint or out of a perverse desire for self-torture, you will be filled with bitter secret regret for what you have done, and the renunciation will be false and will bring you no enlightenment.

What, exactly, is meant by mental renunciation? We are told that we must mentally surrender all our possessions to God, and receive them back from him only on trust, as a workman receives tools from an employer on condition that they are to be used in the employer's service. It may be objected that this kind of renunciation is nothing but a token, a kind of charming poetic fancy. And yet this "fancy" can produce a quality of character which is apparent to the most materialistically-minded observer. We have all met men and women who do their jobs with a selfless devotion which sets them apart from the rest of us. We are accustomed to speak of such people as "dedicated," without pausing to ask ourselves in what it is that their dedication consists. If we get to know one of them well, we may even find that his or her dedicated attitude of mind has not been consciously cultivated or willed, or inspired by any religious beliefs; it is, as one says, "natural." And this brings us to the edge of that tremendous mystery we call Personality—a mystery to which the theory of reincarnation seems to provide one of the most satisfactory keys.

Nonattachment seems the best translation of the Sanskrit word used in the Gita, yet in our language it has misleading associations. It suggests coldness and indifference and a fatalistic outlook. One can best appreciate its true meaning by considering its opposite. In general, mankind almost always acts with attachment—that is to say, with fear and desire; desire for a certain result and fear that this result will not be obtained. Action produces all kinds of "fruits"—sweet, bitter or blended in flavor—everything, from a beautiful wife and family, a million dollars and an international reputation, to poverty, disease and public disgrace. Attachment, therefore, means bondage to any and all of these things. One can be in bondage to failure just as much as to success. Dwelling on mistakes and humiliations is just as egotistical as dwelling on achievements and triumphs.

On the chain of attachment the padlock, so to speak, is egotism. And what is egotism? My obstinate belief that I am some particular somebody—Mr. Jones, Mademoiselle Dupont—rather than the Atman. Get the padlock open and you have achieved nonattachment. You now know that you are the Atman and that every action is done for the sake of the Atman alone. Work has become sacramental. No fruits of it are desired, no consequences are feared. The work is its own reward; and as long as it is done to the very best of one's ability, that reward can never be withheld. There are, of course, many degrees of nonattachment; it grows by practice, and as it grows and the sense of the Atman's presence increases, the need for further action will gradually fall away from us. The Law of Karma will cease to operate, and we shall be set free from the cycle of birth, death and rebirth.

It follows therefore, theoretically at least, that *every* action —under certain circumstances and for certain individuals— may be a steppingstone to spiritual growth, *if* it is done in the spirit of nonattachment. This is a shocking thought, but we must accept it in principle if we are to accept the Gita's teaching. All good and evil is relative to the individual point of growth. For each individual, certain acts are absolutely wrong. Probably there are acts which are absolutely wrong or absolutely right for every individual alive on earth today. But, from the highest viewpoint, there can be neither good nor evil.

> The Lord is everywhere
> And always perfect:
> What does he care for man's sin
> Or the righteousness of man?

Because Krishna is speaking as God, he can take this attitude, and advise Arjuna to fight. Because Arjuna has reached this particular stage in his development, he can kill his enemies and actually be doing his duty.

There is no question, here, of doing evil that good may come. The Gita does not countenance this kind of opportunism. Arjuna is to do the best he knows at this moment, in order that he may later pass beyond that best to better. Later, through the practice of nonattachment, his responsibilities as a leader and warrior will fall away from him; and when that happens it will have become wrong for him to fight or to do any act of violence. Doing the evil you know to be evil will never bring good. It will lead only to more evil, more attachment, more ignorance.

So the Gita neither sanctions war nor condemns it. Regarding no action as of absolute universal value, for good or for evil, it cannot possibly do either. Its teaching should warn us not to dare to judge others. And how can we ever prescribe our neighbor's duty when it is so hard for us to know our own? After much self-analysis, you may decide that your own scruples are genuine and that you can wholeheartedly take your stand as a pacifist— though the decision is certainly difficult enough, with no Krishna to tell you your duty. But the pacifist must respect Arjuna, just as Arjuna must respect the pacifist. Both are going toward the same goal, if they are really sincere. There is an underlying solidarity between them, if each one follows without compromise the path upon which he finds himself. For we can only help others to do their nature's duty by doing what we ourselves believe to be right. It is the one truly disinterested social act.

OUR WORK on the Gita was, for me, not only a literary problem but an education in Vedanta Philosophy. Even if the result had not been intended for publication, I should have felt that every moment of it was worthwhile. For the slow thoroughgoing process of translating a text—considering all the significance of each word and often spending a day on three or four verses—is the ideal way to study, *if* you have a teacher like Prabhavananda. The Swami's English was fluent and his knowledge of Sanskrit equally good. As regards the latter, he had an advantage in being a Bengali—for the Bengali language has about the same relation to Sanskrit as modern Greek has to classical Greek. Sanskrit is no longer spoken, except when monks, priests or scholars from different parts of India use it as their only common language, just as an Irish Catholic priest might talk to a German priest in Latin. At that time, I knew no Sanskrit whatsoever; even today I have absolutely no knowledge of its grammar and could easily write down my little vocabulary on one side of a post card. My share in the collaboration was therefore secondary. Prabhavananda told me the meaning of a phrase; we then considered how this meaning could best be conveyed in English.

The problem was more difficult than it sounds, because the Gita itself is a much more complex work than it at first appears to be. Although it is relatively short, it is not a uniform whole—either from a philosophical or a literary standpoint. Indeed, it is as various as the Bible. There is no need to prove this point by claiming, as some scholars have done, that certain portions of it may have been added later; that is a vexed question and anyhow immaterial. That the existing version of the Gita has at least four distinct aspects, any careful reader can see for himself.

Unlike the Bible, the Gita is all in verse, but this is not to say that it is all good poetry. Some of the material is essentially poetic, but other parts of it have merely been forced into verse-form, no doubt in order to make them easier to memorize. In

India today, there are still many people who can recite the whole Gita by heart. It is often chanted or read in its entirety at important religious festivals.

The Gita can be said to be partly an epic, partly a prophetic vision, partly a gospel, partly a philosophical exposition.

As I have already said, it is constructed to fit into an epic poem; its opening chapter continues in the mood of the Mahabharata, with a background of menacing war-trumpets. The narrative style is still that of the classical epic:

"Then Krishna, subduer of the senses, thus requested by Arjuna, the conqueror of sloth, drove that most splendid of chariots into a place between the two armies, confronting Bhisma, Drona and all those other rulers of the earth. And he said: 'O Prince, behold the assembled Kurus!' "

Yet in the very next chapter, Krishna talks like this: "I have explained to you the true nature of the Atman. Now listen to the method of Karma Yoga . . . ." This is certainly not the tone of an epic character; it is a teacher of philosophy addressing his pupil.

Then again, in the eleventh chapter, we have poetry in the prophetic manner; something akin to the visions of Isaiah and the Book of Revelations. Krishna is transfigured and appears to Arjuna in his true nature, as Lord of the Universe: ". . . speaking from unnumerable mouths, seeing with a myriad eyes, of many marvelous aspects, adorned with countless divine ornaments, brandishing all kinds of heavenly weapons, wearing celestial garlands and the raiment of paradise, anointed with perfumes of heavenly fragrance, full of revelations, resplendent, boundless, of ubiquitous regard. Suppose a thousand suns should rise together into the sky: such is the glory of the Shape of Infinite God."

And lastly, scattered throughout the book, we find passages of dialogue which seem almost dateless in their simplicity, belonging to no particular epoch. As in the Christian Gospel, man and incarnate God speak together as friend to friend:

Arjuna: "When a man goes astray from the path to Brahman, he has missed both lives, the worldly and the spiritual. He has no support anywhere. Is he not lost, as a broken cloud is lost in the sky?"

Krishna: "No, my son. That man is not lost, either in this world or the next. No one who seeks Brahman ever comes to an evil end."

How is the translator to render these different aspects of the Gita and reconcile them with each other? It is clear that no single uniform style will be adequate. Basic English cannot deal with the ornateness of the poetic passages, poetic language cannot convey the precise meanings of the philosophical terms, academic language is too awkward for the directness of the colloquial passages. And besides, Sanskrit differs radically from modern English. The Gita is phrased with the terseness of a telegram. It is full of technical philosophic words for which we have often no direct equivalent. And it is based upon a very definite conception of the universe which is implicit in its statements and must be explained to the modern reader. Here are some of the key words in the Gita's vocabulary. Each one is a problem for the translator.

Brahman is the Reality in its universal aspect, as opposed to the *Atman* which is the Reality within ourselves. The Reality is always the Reality, one and undivided; these two words merely designate two viewpoints from which it can be considered. Look inward and you see the Atman, look outward and you see Brahman; but Atman and Brahman are really one . . . . Very well, now how are you going to translate? If you call Brahman "God," you are apt to create a misunderstanding—at least in the mind of any Christian or Jew. For "God" is naturally associated by them with the Jehovah of the Old Testament, and Jehovah is God-with-attributes; He is alternately stern and merciful, He wills certain events, He favors the Children of Israel. There is a word in Sanskrit for God-with-attributes; it is *Ishwara.* But Brahman is the Reality without attributes, without will, without moods. It is Brahman seen within Maya, that appears as Ishwara. If you translate Brahman as "The Reality" or "The Absolute," you still have to explain what you mean; these overworked words have become so imprecise. If you use "The Godhead," as has been done in translations from Meister Eckhart, you seem nearer to a definition, since the dictionary says it means "the essential being of God." But somehow this starkly mediaeval word sounds odd and unfitting on the lips of Krishna.

The Atman, it has been said, is the Reality within ourselves. But when one searches for a single English word to say this, it cannot be found, because Christianity does not quite accept this concept. "Soul" is out of the question; the soul is not God. "Spirit" is utterly vague. Many translators call the Atman "The Self"; but this word has unfortunate associations with "selfishness." Moreover, there are certain passages in which the translator is then forced to speak of the Self with a big S meaning the Atman and the self with a small s meaning the personal ego; a distinction which is lost when the words are read aloud. And an occasionally unavoidable use of the possessive form produces the horrible combination "his Self." You can more or less adequately describe the Atman as "God Immanent" and Brahman as "God Transcendent," but these phrases are too awkward for frequent repetition and they have the dryness of Victorian theology.

The meanings of the word *karma* have already been discussed. Here, the translator cannot hope to find absolute equivalents. Even in its primary meaning, karma cannot always be translated by the same word; one has to alternate between "action" and "work" according to the context. As for the secondary meaning of karma, what is the use of translating it as "the effect of a deed"? The expression is falsely simple; further explanation is absolutely necessary. And the Law of Karma— well, how is any Western reader to know what that is, until he has been told in at least one fairly long sentence?

Explanation at length is also unavoidable in dealing with the very important words *Prakriti* and *Maya*. It has been said that Brahman is without attributes. What, then, is the relation of Brahman to the universe? Brahman cannot be said to create, preserve or destroy. It is the power or effect of Brahman—other than Brahman yet inseparable from Brahman, just as heat is inseparable from fire—which forms the stuff of all mind and matter. This power of Brahman is called Prakriti. Since Prakriti is by definition coexistent with Brahman, the universe must also be thought of as being without beginning or end—though it may pass through phases of potentiality and expression, during which it seems to be alternately created and destroyed. Each of us has, so to speak, one foot in the absolute and one in the relative; our nature is the Atman, our substance is Prakriti. Enlightenment is the recognition of a situation which already exists, namely that we are the Atman essentially and Prakriti only relatively. Nevertheless, Prakriti cannot be said to be unreal. Brahman lends it a relative reality. This universe and Ishwara its master are related to Brahman inseparably. The many aspects of Ishwara, God-within-the-universe, are projected by the one Brahman.

And so we come to Maya—almost the only Sanskrit word which many people know, or believe they know. They believe it means "illusion," and they are wrong. Actually, the words Maya and Prakriti are interchangeable. They do not *mean* illusion, but from the absolute viewpoint they *are* illusion; since, when Brahman is known, Prakriti is seen to have only a relative existence. Some translators—the kind who are determined to translate at any cost—have rendered Prakriti as "Nature" or "Primordial Matter." This is the best way to confirm a lazy reader in his laziness. "Ah yes—Nature," he murmurs to himself and passes on, without having made the least effort to understand what the term is being used to mean.

Finally, there are the three *Gunas; sattwa, rajas* and *tamas.* Modern science tells us that matter is energy. The cosmology of Vedanta also contains this concept. Prakriti is said to be composed of three gunas, or forces. During a phase of potentiality—when the universe has been apparently destroyed and is actually in a "seed-state"—these gunas are in perfect equilibrium, and Prakriti is just undifferentiated "matter-stuff." What we call creation is the upsetting of this equilibrium. The gunas forthwith begin to enter into an ever increasing variety of combinations which are the various forms of mind and matter that make up the universe during its phases of expression. The universe continues to develop in this manner until it can, as it were, no longer bear the burden of its own complexity; at this point it dissolves, returning to its potential phase, and thus to ultimate rebirth. Such is the unending cyclic process.

Each of the three gunas has a character, and it is the exact proportion to which each of the three is present in any given object that determines the nature of that object. One guna is of course always predominant over the others, in order that disequilibrium may be maintained; since without disequilibrium there can be no expression.

In the physical sphere, sattwa embodies all that is pure and fine, rajas embodies violence and movement, tamas the quality of solidity and resistance. Sattwa, for example, predominates in sunlight, rajas in an erupting volcano, tamas in a block of granite. In the psychological sphere, sattwa expresses itself as tranquillity, purity, calmness; rajas as passion, restlessness, aggressive activity; tamas as stupidity, laziness, inertia. The gunas also represent the three stages in the evolution of any particular entity. Sattwa is the essence of the form to be realized; tamas is the inherent obstacle to that realization; rajas is the power by which that obstacle is removed and the essential form made manifest. For example, a sculptor gets an idea (sattwa) for a figure of a horse. To make the idea manifest, he needs granite (tamas) and muscular power (rajas). He feels lazy (tamas) but overcomes the laziness by his determination (rajas), and so, in due course, his idea of the horse (sattwa) is given physical expression. From this it is clear that all three gunas are absolutely necessary for any act of creation. Sattwa alone would be just an unrealized idea, rajas without sattwa would be mere undirected energy, rajas without tamas would be like a lever without a fulcrum.

I have taken three paragraphs to explain what the Gunas are—yet there are many translators who offer one-word English equivalents. Here are five different ones, taken from five versions of the Gita: The qualities, the moods, the elements, the strands, the dispositions. And for the individual gunas there is an equal variety of renderings. Sattwa is translated as purity, goodness, truth; rajas as fieriness, passion, greed; tamas as ignorance, dullness, gloom. Not one of these is absolutely wrong; not one is right in all possible contexts, physical and psychological. What, for example, is the uninitiated reader to understand by the goodness of x-rays, the greed of a volcano or the gloom of a table? And if we use different words to suit different contexts, we can no longer pretend to have an exact terminology with which to express the Gita's teaching.

There is, of course, an alternative: to decide that certain much-used terms must remain in the original Sanskrit and be explained in footnotes or an appendix. This is probably the lesser evil. But the translator must keep the Sanskrit down to a minimum. There are all too many versions which contain verses like this:

"Those who know Me with the *Adhibhuta,* the *Adhidaiva,* and the *Adhiyajna,* continue to know me even at the time of death, steadfast in mind."

Then, again, there is the snare of literalness. I have already remarked that Sanskrit differs greatly in its construction from English. A certain degree of paraphrase would seem to be absolutely necessary, but a very subtle line divides paraphrase from comment and exposition. The translator must decide just how far he can go. If he does not go far enough, he will produce something like the last radio message from a sinking ship: "By the intellect set in patience; mind placed in the Self; making by degrees should attain quietude; not even anything should think."

*   *   *

Afterword

AT THIS POINT, my original manuscript ends, except for half a dozen pages which were intended to form a bridge passage between this autobiographical introduction and the beginning of the Ramakrishna biography proper.

Now I will add a few words in conclusion.

THE LONGER I remained in contact with Prabhavananda and the Vedanta society, the more clearly I understood that religion—at any rate for a person of my temperament—must mean primarily a relationship: a relationship leading at long last to direct union with the Atman; a relationship for the time being with some individual who can give you a dim glimpse of the Atman within him, simply by being what he is. Such an individual doesn't have to be perfect. But he must have no pretenses; he must be, at all times, neither more nor less than himself. If there is this clarity in his character, then you can look into him, as it were, and, very occasionally, get a glimpse of the something-else, the element which is not-he, not his personality, not his individual nature. And then you can begin to have faith in his faith. You can feel that he is holding you, like a rock-climber on a rope, just as he himself is being held by the rope that goes on up above him. That is what the disciple demands of the guru. It is a tremendous demand.

I HAVE described the state of near-despair in which I first made contact with Vedanta, through Gerald Heard and Prabhavananda, in 1939. Some readers may think that what I have written about this amounts to a very damaging admission. They may say: "If you were so desperate at the time, what was your conversion really worth? Weren't you simply grasping at the nearest straw? Weren't you in the mood to believe in anyone and anything?"

I am not concerned, here, with any apology for my own thoughts and actions; but I owe it to the reader to reassure him, on general principles. So I will make this answer: Yes—it is quite true that I didn't enter upon this new phase of my life in a mood of critical objectivity. I wasn't calm. I was deeply disturbed. It is arguable that I was ready to clutch at straws, and perhaps to put my trust in charlatans, if only they could offer me some sense of security, however specious. Let me admit all that . . . . But, if you feel worried, because it seems to invalidate what I have written about Vedanta and to rule me out as a reliable witness, then please consider—I am writing these words more than twenty-three years later. Can one keep afloat for twenty-three years on a straw?

January 1963